ARTS AND CRAFTS
DISCOVERY UNITS

- Let's Discover TISSUE

  Let's Discover Crayon

  Let's Discover Watercolor

  Let's Discover Paper

  Let's Discover Puppets

  Let's Discover Mobiles

  Let's Discover Tempera

  Let's Discover Printing

  Let's Discover Papier-Mache

  Let's Discover Weaving

LET'S DISCOVER TISSUE

Jenean Romberg

Arts and Crafts Discovery Units

The Center for Applied Research in Education, Inc.
521 Fifth Avenue, New York, N.Y. 10017

Library of Congress Cataloging in Publication Data

Romberg, Jenean.
  Let's discover tissue

    (Her Arts and Crafts discovery units, 2)
    1. Paper work. 2. Tissue paper.
3. Activity programs in education. I. Title.
NK70.R65   372.5'044   73-15953
ISBN 0-87628-530-2

PRINTED IN THE UNITED STATES OF AMERICA

Let's Discover . . .

Crayons . . . paper . . . paint . . . paste . . . scissors . . . the list of materials available for creative activities is endless. But it makes little difference how many exciting materials are available if we do not know how to use them and do not realize their potential. It is important to take the time to explore the uses and limitations of different media, materials, and techniques, become skillful in their uses, and learn what we, personally, can or cannot do.

The LET'S DISCOVER . . . series provides a broad exploration of basic materials, utilizing a wide variety of tools and techniques as well as manipulative and organizational skills. Each of its ten parts includes dozens of activities selected to meet special moods and occasions and sequentially organized to allow a progression from very simple techniques in one media, to more complex techniques involving several media. The techniques are designed to enable anyone to achieve fascinating and intriguing effects so that those important "initial" experiences with a particular medium are positive and rewarding.

It is natural for each of us to want to make things, to experiment and explore. After gaining confidence and knowledge we then feel secure enough to be inventive, to express individual ideas, take pride and gain satisfaction in creativity. By choosing and creating colors, textures, and shapes, we share something of ourselves with others.

Let's explore, experiment, create!

Jenean Romberg

ACKNOWLEDGMENTS

With love and thanks to my sister, Sandy Kincaid, and my aunt, Marie V. Howes, for their "unending patient help" in preparing these manuscripts.

contents...

about tissue...

Hurray for tissue—that gossamer, brilliantly-hued material that seems to come from the very land of enchantment! So many wonderful experiences can evolve from this exciting medium. Tissue is vivid, translucent, light in weight, durable and flexible. Persons of all age levels work with it with great enthusiasm and success. It can be pasted, glued, starched, crumpled, stuffed, torn, wet and cut. Overlapping can be done successfully because of its great translucent quality and amazing new colors can be achieved.

The magic of blending and creating different hues and values inspires the imagination of children. Since tissue is so very light-weight and easy to manipulate, crumpling and pasting the tissue can provide two- and three-dimensional effects. It lends itself to many different techniques and combines well with other media. The opportunities are endless.

In this book we will explore the many exciting possibilities in the world of tissue, from very simple experiences such as overlapping colors and creating the secondary colors to making wall plaques. Sometimes there will be several variations of the same technique, each involving a little more skill and coordination, while other projects will only have one example with suggestions for variations. There has been no attempt to dictate how or what one is to draw.

The titles and examples are merely hints or suggestions for motivation. The techniques are designed to enable anyone to achieve fascinating and intriguing effects. So begin right away—there's nothing to fear, and there's great fun in store for all!

WELCOME TO THE WORLD OF TISSUE!

techniques with tissue...

The following techniques will be used in the tissue activities in this book. Here is a brief summary of each:

- tearing: do several pieces at one time as tissue paper is very light-weight; it will be easier to control.

- cutting: free-form, symmetrical shapes on the fold.

- applying tissue to other surfaces:

  liquid starch—easiest and least expensive to use as an adhesive, adheres to most surfaces; apply with use of soft bristle paint brush, putting starch underneath and on top of each piece of tissue.

  white glue—provides a durable, glossy, hard finish to completed project; expensive, sometimes too thick to work with.

  white glue mixture—consists of two parts white glue to one part water; gives a hard, waterproof, fairly glossy surface to completed project.

- tissue transparencies—tissue paper between two layers of cut-out construction paper; hung or placed so the light can shine through the tissue paper.

- laminated tissue—torn or cut pieces of tissue paper placed between two layers of wax paper and ironed with a warm iron; the wax melts and bonds all together.

- layered tissue—cut or torn pieces of tissue paper are applied to a piece of wax paper with liquid starch, each piece overlapping, several layers thick. When dry, the wax paper is peeled away and the pieces of tissue paper adhere, creating one sheet of paper.

It is often desirable to add a protective durable finish to a completed project. The following materials can be used:

- polymer gloss medium—gives a hard, durable, waterproof surface to finished project; clean-up is easy as brushes can be cleaned with water. It looks like white glue but dries to a clear finish.

- shellac/varnish—gives a high-gloss, durable, waterproof finish to completed project; often preferred because of the high-gloss finish. It is difficult to clean-up; special thinners and brush cleaners are needed.

- clear plastic spray—quick and easy to use, especially nice for flatwork projects; doesn't give a real high gloss to project, just a protective covering.

keeping art happy...
format~

—each activity begins with a list of materials needed for each individual.

—all supplies are generally those available in the schools, local art shops, easy to find or inexpensive.

—all paper sizes are divisible into 12 x 18 or 20 x 30 sheets of tissue paper to eliminate the overflowing "scrap box" which eventually ends up in the trash. Sometimes, however, there will be a need for scraps, so do have a box or drawer for paper scraps of all kinds.

—directions are simple and to the point, with illustrations to demonstrate each step while still allowing for the greatest freedom of individual expression.

—at the end of each activity there is an idea for a variation of the project, a bulletin board idea, or an important suggestion for making things go easier.

—almost all of the projects, with a little adaptation or simplification, can be used with any age level.

—the illustrations and captions for each activity are simply for suggestion. Show samples, demonstrate, and give examples, but then let students go from there and they will . . . beautifully.

—the activities and their variations do not necessarily need to be taught in sequence.

The following materials are needed to do the activities in this book:

tissue paper, all colors	crayons
construction paper, all colors	marking pens
white drawing paper	scissors
cardboard or chipboard	paint brushes: #6, #10, #12 watercolor
aluminum foil	1–2″ stiff bristle
wax paper	iron
newspapers	balloons
liquid starch	paper towels
small containers	needle and thread
(milk cartons are best)	roving, yarn
coat hangers	sequins, glitter

liquid bleach
q-tips
white glue
paste

dried beans, peas, cereals
pieces of wood for wall plaques

shellac, varnish, polymer gloss medium or clear
plastic spray for protective coverings

Make a collection of things that have textured surfaces for crayon rubbings such as:

leaves	string	fine grasses	cutouts	textured fabric
burlap	window screen	sandpaper		waffle-weave fabric
rough leather		cheese grater		corrugated paper

Save all tissue scraps! They are marvelous for layered tissue projects as well as free-form collages and other projects.

Be prepared to have the colors of tissue bleed; when a project is completed go over the surface with a wide brush, making the strokes all one way. This will even out the color and when dry give the background a "watercolor" look.

White glue and white glue mixtures will work well for adhering tissue to other surfaces but be sure to wash brushes thoroughly when through.

Milk cartons are excellent for individual containers for starch as they're easy to get, and do not tip over easily.

Keep a box with 3″ and 5″ squares of tissue paper of all colors on hand. Many activities call for this size of tissue and in an emergency it will be waiting.

getting ready - go!

—always have the materials ready!

—try the activity yourself before presenting it; you will be more aware of the techniques and the knowledge needed as well as the pitfalls to be avoided.

—do demonstrate. Your free use of materials and your approach will encourage others; care, use of materials, and basic skills can be demonstrated at the same time.

—don't be afraid to have a demonstration turn out a failure; if it does, discuss why.

—allow plenty of time in which to complete each project; divide into two or more working periods if necessary.

—encourage individuality and originality; remind students not to be "cameras."

—encourage the student to discover things for himself; to be resourceful.

—allow the students to share their work with each other either while they are working or when the activity is completed. It's exciting and often motivating to see what others are doing.

—display the work of all students; encourage students to exhibit their work so that everyone can enjoy it.

—MOST OF ALL MAKE ART A HAPPY HAPPENING!

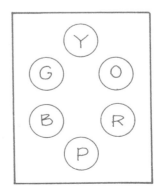

MATERIALS:

3″ squares of tissue, 3 pieces
each of red, blue, and yellow

(1) 12″ x 18″ white construction paper

liquid starch in a small container

soft bristle brush and scissors

newspaper for working surface

DISCOVERY STEPS:

1. Fold the 3″ squares of tissue paper in half, all 3 pieces of a color together. Trim off the open corners to make circles.

2. Fold the 12″ x 18″ white construction paper in half, widthwise.

3. On one half of the white construction paper, place the primary colors, red, yellow, and blue; one circle of each color in the order shown. Put a circle of starch on the white paper with the paint brush, lay on the tissue circles and then cover the tissue with starch.

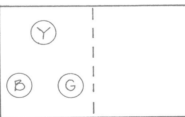

4. In the spaces between the primary colors put the other tissue circles in the order shown below to produce the secondary colors, orange, violet, and green.

between: red and yellow: starch, red, and
then yellow
blue and red: starch, blue, and
then red
yellow and blue: starch, blue, and
then yellow

Be sure to put starch under and over each piece of tissue.

5. On the other half of the white construction paper use the tissue scraps to make a design. Paint the paper with starch and lay on the tissue pieces, overlapping colors to make the secondary colors. Put starch over and under each piece of tissue.

tissue bottles

MATERIALS:

(1) 9″ x 12″ white construction paper

(1) 6″ x 6″ square of tissue paper of each color: red, yellow, blue

liquid starch in a small container

scissors, paint brush, black crayon

newspaper for working surface

DISCOVERY STEPS:

1. Cut each of the three pieces of tissue paper into a different shape bottle. The tissue paper can be folded as illustrated and the shape cut on the fold.

2. Using the paint brush, cover the entire piece of white paper with liquid starch.

3. Arrange the tissue bottles on the white paper in the following order so that the secondary contrasts will show through the translucence of the bottles:

   1. red

   2. yellow overlapping red

   3. blue overlapping yellow and red

   As each shape is placed on the white paper, apply a coat of starch, making sure not to go over the edges.

4. When the tissue bottles are dry, outline the shapes with black crayon.

VARIATIONS: Cut the 6″ squares into various geometric shapes; put on white paper with starch, overlapping shapes and colors to create the secondary colors. When dry, outline with black crayon.

tissue plaids

MATERIALS:

(1) 9″ x 12″ white construction paper

pre-cut strips of tissue paper of
various widths

liquid starch in a small container

paint brush, scissors

newspaper for working surface

PREPARATION:

Place three or four different color sheets of tissue paper in a single stack. Using the
paper cutter, cut into ½″, ¼″, ¾″, 1″ and 1½″ strips.

DISCOVERY STEPS:

1. Place the white construction paper on newspaper. Paint the entire surface with a
   coat of liquid starch.

2. Lay on horizontal strips, three or more of each color. Vary widths and spaces
   between the strips. Let the ends stick over the edge. Fill the brush with starch and
   paint the entire surface horizontally.

3. Lay on the vertical strips, three or more of each color. Vary the widths of the strips
   and the spaces between. Let the ends stick over the edge. Fill the brush with starch
   and paint the entire surface vertically.

4. When dry, trim off the ends of the tissue paper.

SUGGESTIONS: These make beautiful cards, book or folder covers, and also are very
striking when mounted on paper of a complementary color.

autumn leaves

MATERIALS:

(1) 9″ x 12″ white construction paper

(2 each) 5″ squares of red, yellow, orange and tan tissue paper

liquid starch in a small container

soft bristle brush and scissors

pencil, 4½″ x 6″ pieces of newsprint

DISCOVERY STEPS:

1. Tear or cut the tissue paper squares into small pieces.

2. Paint the entire surface of the white drawing paper with liquid starch. Place small pieces of tissue paper on the white paper, one at a time. Paint over each piece with liquid starch. Mix the colors, overlapping pieces. Cover entire paper. Let dry.

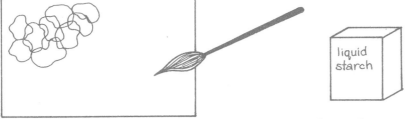

3. Fold the pieces of newsprint and on each draw half a leaf centered on the fold. Cut out. These will be used as patterns.

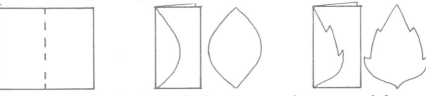

4. When the tissue paper is dry lay the leaf patterns on the paper and draw around them with the pencil. Cut out. Make as many as possible different sizes. Scraps may be used for letters for captions, etc.

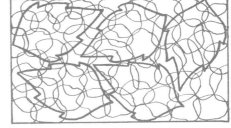

5. The leaves can be glued to a dried branch, put on the bulletin board or hung as a mobile.

VARIATION: Can also be done on wax paper for transparent leaves to hang in windows.

action people

MATERIALS:

piece of the classified section of
newspaper cut 12″ x 18″ or 9″ x 12″

tissue paper, any colors desired

liquid starch in a small container

wide brush

black crayon

DISCOVERY STEPS:

1. Tear tissue paper into medium-size pieces.

2. Paint the newspaper with liquid starch and lay on pieces of tissue paper. As you put down each piece of tissue paper cover it with a coat of starch. Remind the students that they don't need to cover every bit of the newspaper with tissue paper.

3. Let dry. (This will be a two-day or two-part project.)

4. Using the black crayon, make five dots on the paper far apart. Make stick figures running, jumping, skipping and so forth: make one dot the head, draw hands and feet at the other dots, then connect with lines for the body.

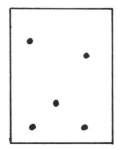 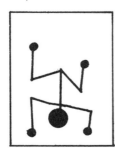 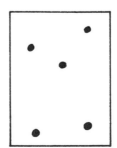

VARIATIONS: Geometric shapes, snowflakes, patterns, or cut letters all made of tissue look delightful with the classified sections of the newspaper as background.

tissue people

MATERIALS:

9″ x 12″ light orange tissue
(for parts of body)

all sizes of scraps of bright
colored tissue for clothes

liquid starch in small container

soft bristle brush

9″ x 12″ white construction paper

DISCOVERY STEPS:

1. Using the light orange tissue paper, tear out the parts of the body.

2. Cover the white construction paper with liquid starch using the paint brush. Lay on the parts of the body, placing the head and torso first and then putting on the arms and legs so that they show action.

3. Put a coat of starch on top of each part of the body.

4. Using the colored tissue paper tear out clothes, hair and any other details. Lay over the parts of the body and cover with starch.

5. The following illustrations show easy ways to cut clothes.

an Indian Chief

MATERIALS:

(1) 9″ x 12″ white drawing paper

(1) 4½″ x 6″ yellow or tan tissue

(1) 4½″ x 6″ brown tissue paper

tissue scraps, all colors

soft bristle brush

liquid starch in a small container

(1) 9″ x 12″ black construction paper

DISCOVERY STEPS:

1. Tear away edges of the yellow or tan tissue paper to create the face. Use the 4½″ x 6″ brown tissue paper to make hair.

2. Using the scraps of tissue paper, tear out facial features and feathers for the head-dress. Use many colors for the feathers.

3. Using the paint brush, cover the entire surface of the white paper with liquid starch. Place the face shape in the middle or just below the middle of the paper. Cover with starch. Add the hair and facial features. Add feathers, remembering to overlap to create new colors.

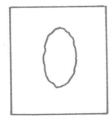 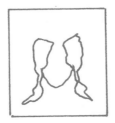 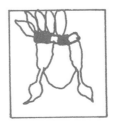

4. When the project is dry black crayon can be used to outline and/or accent the various shapes.

MAKING THE FRAME: Fold the 9″ x 12″ black construction paper in half lengthwise. Tear out the center section as shown, leaving a one-inch border.

cascading shapes

MATERIALS:

(6) 5″ x 5″ squares of colored tissue paper, 2 each of 3 colors

scissors

soft bristle brush

liquid starch in small container

(1) 6″ x 18″ white drawing paper

DISCOVERY STEPS:

1. Fold the tissue pieces of each color together and cut out half-a-shape on the fold. These can be lightly penciled on the tissue paper before cutting if desired. Some suggested shapes:

2. Arrange the shapes on the white paper; experiment with different arrangements, turn them at all angles, some overlapping. Tissue scraps can be added as well.

3. Remove pieces from white paper. Using the soft bristle paint brush, cover the white paper with a coat of liquid starch. Lay shapes on one at a time, covering each piece separately with starch before adding another.

4. When all the shapes are on, fill the brush with starch and go over the whole paper with straight, even strokes, going from edge to edge either horizontally or vertically. This will spread out and even up any color that has bled from the tissue paper and does create a very interesting effect.

MATERIALS:

over and over

12″ x 18″ grey bogus paper

4″ x 4″ squares of tissue paper, 10 pieces each of three colors

liquid starch

small container for starch

paint brush

scissors

black crayon

DISCOVERY STEPS:

1. Fold the 4″ x 4″ tissue squares in half. Do several at one time. Cut out many sizes and shapes on the fold.

2. Using the paint brush, apply liquid starch to the grey bogus paper. Lay tissue shapes on, covering each with liquid starch. Remember to overlap the shapes.

3. When dry outline the shapes with black crayon, add lines, dots, etc.

VARIATION: Calico Designs—Cut various size squares and rectangles; overlap shapes when applying to white paper. Add details with black crayon.

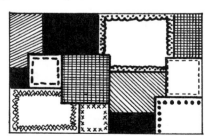

MATERIALS:

(4) 5″ x 5″ squares of light green and yellow tissue paper

(2) 5″ x 5″ squares of dark-colored tissue paper (for flowers)

(2) 5″ x 5″ squares of dark green tissue paper

scissors

liquid starch and paint brush

9″ x 12″ lime green construction paper

DISCOVERY STEPS:

1. Tear the light green and yellow tissue into small pieces.

2. Put a coat of starch over the lime green construction paper with the paint brush. Then put the light green and yellow pieces of tissue paper all over the green paper. Cover each piece of tissue paper with starch. This will make the background for the garden.

3. Cut one dark green square into thin strips for stems. Fold the other piece into fourths and then fold once more. Cut out a leaf shape. This will make 8 leaves.

4. Lay stems and leaves on the background while it is still wet. Lay some of the stems at angles so that the flowers look like they are moving. Then using the tip of the brush, carefully apply starch to these, just on the tissue so the color doesn't run.

5. Cut out flowers all at the same time by folding both pieces of tissue together in fourths.

6. Put the flowers on top of the stems and cover carefully with starch.

MATERIALS:

5″ x 5″ dark blue tissue paper (1)

5″ x 5″ white tissue paper (3)

5″ x 5″ squares tissue paper of different colors (4)

scissors

liquid starch

9″ x 12″ light blue construction paper

DISCOVERY STEPS:

1. Tear the white and dark blue tissue into pieces.

2. Put a little starch all over the light blue construction paper and then lay the white and dark blue tissue on, one piece at a time, overlapping and covering each with starch. This will make sky and background.

3. Cut the colored squares of tissue into different sizes of squares, rectangles, triangles, and circles. Put them together to make houses and buildings. Lay them out along the top of the working surface.

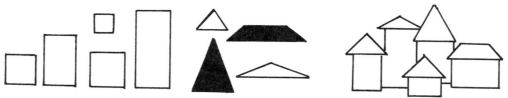

4. Place the houses over the background on the construction paper. This will still be wet, so lay each piece carefully and then cover with starch before adding another. Put starch just on the pieces so the colors don't run.

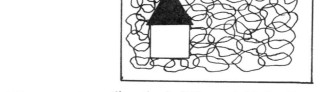

5. The following day when it is dry, use crayon to outline the buildings. Add details such as T.V. antennae, tiny people, cars, and so forth.

MATERIALS:

(1) 9″ x 12″ brown construction paper

(1) 12″ x 18″ white construction paper

tissue paper, fall colors, torn
into medium-size pieces

small container of liquid starch

paint brush and paper towel

scissors and pencil

DISCOVERY STEPS:

1. Lay the 12″ x 18″ piece of white construction paper on top of newspaper. Using the paint brush, cover the entire surface of the paper with liquid starch. Lay on the torn pieces of tissue paper, one at a time, and cover with starch. Cover the entire paper with tissue. Let dry overnight in a flat area.

2. Fold the 9″ x 12″ brown construction paper in half, lengthwise. Draw half a tree on the fold. The older the students are the more detailed this can be.

3. Cut out the tree. Remind the students to keep the tree in one piece. Follow the pencil line and cut carefully.

4. Fold the tissue-covered paper in half, widthwise. Paste or glue the cut-out tree on one half and the outline on the other side of the paper. This creates a positive-negative picture.

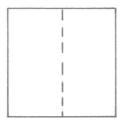 

VARIATIONS: Any symmetrical shape cut on the fold can be used to create positive-negative designs as shown in these examples.

 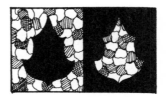

a cornucopia

MATERIALS:

tissue paper (brown, purple, red, blue, green, orange, yellow)

(1) 9″ x 12″ newsprint

(1) 9″ x 12″ white construction paper

small container of liquid starch

paint brush, scissors and pencil

DISCOVERY STEPS:

1. Cut cornucopia out of brown tissue paper and cut various fruit shapes from the other colors of tissue paper.

2. Arrange the design on the 9″ x 12″ piece of newsprint.

3. Paint the white construction paper with liquid starch. Move the arrangement from the newsprint to the white paper, one piece at a time. Go over the top of each piece lightly with starch. Be careful not to go over the edges so the colors won't run.

 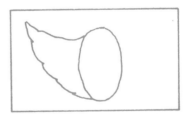

4. Outline the shapes of the fruit and cornucopia with back crayon after it is dry. The colors of the tissue may have run just a bit and this makes it more interesting; just outline the original shapes of the fruit.

VARIATIONS: This technique is applicable to any picture. After doing this activity so the process is understood, put all sorts of tissue scraps and paper out to create seasonal pictures, still-lifes and designs. The following are examples:

MATERIALS:

(1) 9″ x 12″ white drawing paper

small container of liquid starch

(1 each) 6″ x 6″ tissue: lavender, light green, dark green, light blue, turquoise and purple

scissors

soft bristle paint brush

DISCOVERY STEPS:

1. Cut the 6″ tissue squares into the following shapes:

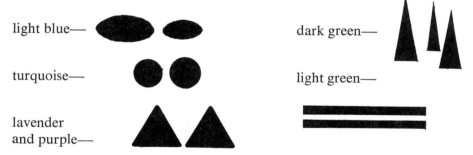

light blue—

turquoise—

lavender and purple—

dark green—

light green—

2. Cover the entire surface of the white construction paper with a coat of liquid starch, using the soft bristle paint brush.

3. Apply the shapes to the white paper in the following sequence, covering each piece of tissue paper with liquid starch, overlapping pieces:

light blue—sky

lavender, purple—mountains

light green—grass
(leave room for lake)

turquoise—lake

dark green—trees

MATERIALS:

(3 each) 5″ x 10″ pieces of red, yellow and orange tissue paper

(1) 5″ x 10″ purple tissue paper

(1) 9″ x 12″ white drawing paper

liquid starch in a small container

soft bristle brush

(1) 6″ x 9″ black construction paper

glue or paste

DISCOVERY STEPS:

1. Tear the 5″ x 10″ strips of purple, red, yellow and orange tissue paper into various width strips. Tear several pieces at one time.

2. Brush the entire surface of the white paper with liquid starch. Apply the strips of tissue paper, overlapping edges of each strip horizontally in the following sequence:

purple

red

orange

yellow

red, orange, yellow

3. While the paper is drying, cut out silhouettes using the black construction paper and scissors.

SUGGESTIONS: trees, buildings, cactus, sailboats, birds, people.

4. Paste or glue the black construction paper silhouettes on top of the tissue paper sunset.

VARIATIONS: The black silhouettes placed on top of the tissue paper sunset can be made with black ink or tempera paint.

MATERIALS:

painting with paper still-lifes

tissue paper, all colors and sizes

heavy white paper such as tagboard, or illustration board cut to desired size

newsprint, same size as white paper

scissors

liquid starch in a small container

newspaper for working surface

DISCOVERY STEPS:

1. Begin with a little pre-planning, sketching some ideas on newsprint with crayon. Show how small sketches can be made on newsprint, trying colors, shapes and arrangements. Then select the still life liked best.

2. Using the various colors and sizes of tissue paper, cut out the shapes desired for the still life. Remember to use scraps wherever possible and to cut on the fold.

3. Arrange the shapes on the piece of newsprint which is the same size as the white paper, remembering to overlap pieces until the arrangement is pleasing.

4. Put starch over the entire surface of the white paper. Transfer the tissue pieces, one at a time, to the white paper, covering each with a layer of starch before adding another. If you don't want the colors to bleed, keep the starch on the tissue only and don't go over the edges.

5. If the colors do bleed when the picture is completed, while still wet, go over the entire surface with a brush full of starch. Paint from edge to edge, making the brush strokes all in one direction.

6. For a glossy finish, spray the finished picture with clear plastic, varnish, shellac, or paint on a coat of gloss medium.

crayon/tissue rubbing

MATERIALS:

5″ squares of tissue paper in autumn colors

fresh leaves with prominent veins

pieces of brown crayon

(1) 9″ x 12″ white construction paper

liquid starch in a small container

paint brush and paper towel

DISCOVERY STEPS:

1. Put a leaf on the table with the vein side up. Place a single piece of tissue paper on top of the leaf and rub over the top of the leaf with the *side* of the crayon. This will pick up the leaf pattern.

2. Do this many times on different colors of tissue paper. Then tear out the leaf shape rubbing on each piece of paper, following the basic shape of the leaf.

3. Using the paint brush, cover the 9″ x 12″ white construction paper with liquid starch. Then, one at a time, lay the tissue leaves on the paper, covering each piece with liquid starch before adding another.

seasonal symbols in 3-D

MATERIALS:

1½″ squares of tissue paper in desired colors

construction paper (9″ x 12″) in appropriate color for shape

paste or glue and scissors

pencil

scraps of construction paper for details

DISCOVERY STEPS:

1. Cut the shape desired out of the colored construction paper. Fold the paper in half widthwise or lengthwise if a symmetrical shape is used. The following are a few suggestions for different seasons of the year:

2. Put some paste or glue in a flat container or on a piece of thick paper.

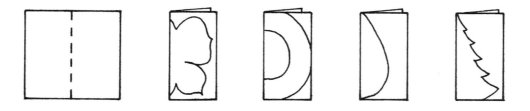

3. Place the forefinger or end of pencil in the center of a tissue square and pinch up the sides. Dip the end of the tissue in paste or glue and then place on the tissue shape. Repeat this step, placing each tissue square close together, until the entire shape is covered. Create designs by using different colors in patterns.

4. When the entire shape is covered with tissue, details can be added with pieces of construction paper, yarn, sequins, glitter and so forth.

a tree for all seasons

MATERIALS:

(1) 9″ x 12″ white construction paper in seasonal color—tan, light blue

thin black or brown tempera paint

a straw

small 1½″ squares of tissue, seasonal colors

scissors

paste or glue

DISCOVERY STEPS:

1. To blow the tree and branches, put a few drops of the very thin tempera paint on the 9″ x 12″ background paper, near the bottom. Blow lightly at the paint with the straw. Move the paper and change the direction in which you blow several different times. Add more paint if necessary. Let dry.

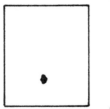  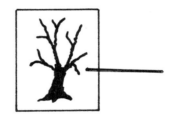

2. When the paint is dry use the tissue paper squares to add the season touches to the tree. Place the forefinger or end of the pencil in the center of a tissue square and pinch up the sides. Dip the end of the tissue in paste or glue and then place on the tree. The following are some suggestions for various times of the year.

fall tree:

background:
  tan
tissue:
  brown
  gold
  yellow
  rust
  orange
  yellow
  red

cherry tree:

background:
  white or
  pink
tissue:
  white
  pink
construction
paper for
cherries

spring tree:

background:
  light blue
tissue:
  white
  pink blossums
  green-leaves

summer tree:

background:
  light blue
tissue:
  shades of
  green

tissue fantasies

MATERIALS:

(1) 12″ x 18″ white drawing paper

(1) 12″ x 18″ tissue paper, light color

crayons, scissors, paint brush

sequins, glitter, yarn, string

tissue scraps

liquid starch in a small container

newspaper

DISCOVERY STEPS:

1. Draw a simple shape in a large pattern on the 12″ x 18″ white drawing paper. Any design or object can be drawn but preferably something with an inner pattern— birds, flowers, butterflies or seasonal objects such as Easter eggs or Christmas ornaments. Complete the design with strong crayon outlines.

  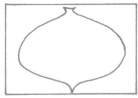 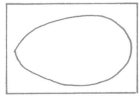

2. Lay a piece of tissue paper about the same size on top of the drawing so that the drawing may be used as a guide.

3. Place long lengths of string in liquid starch and squeeze out excess starch with the fingers. Place the string on the tissue along the outlines of the drawing underneath. When the outline is complete set aside to dry.

4. Add individual touches and decorations with glitter, yarn, sequins, tempera paints, and pieces of tissue paper, attaching with glue or starch.

5. To create a laminated effect, another piece of tissue may be placed on top, covering the surface with starch and putting the second sheet of tissue on top. Put another coat of starch on the second sheet of tissue. Allow to dry thoroughly.

MATERIALS:

a square of any thin paper such as tissue, 9″ x 9″

scissors

DISCOVERY STEPS:

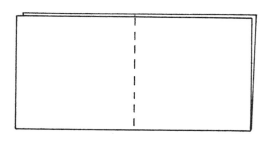

snowflakes

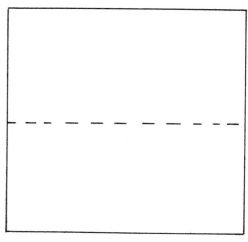

1. Fold the paper in half.

2. Fold in half again so it is 4½″ x 4½″ square.

3. Turn so open edges are at the top. Fold in half diagonally.

4. Fold in half a second time, diagonally.

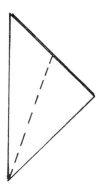

5. Trim off top edges.

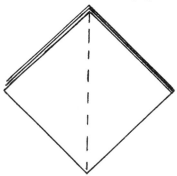

6. Pencil in shapes along folded edges.

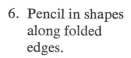

7. Cut out shapes so it looks like this. Open carefully.

snowflake collage

MATERIALS:

(6–8) 5″ squares of tissue paper, assorted colors

(1) 12″ x 18″ white construction paper

scissors, paint brush

liquid starch in a small container

newspaper for working surface

DISCOVERY STEPS:

1. Fold and cut the 5″ tissue squares into snowflakes of various sizes and shapes. See page 44 for instructions on how to cut snowflakes.

2. Place the 12″ x 18″ white construction paper on top of a piece of newspaper.

3. Paint the entire surface of the white construction paper with a layer of liquid starch. Then place the tissue snowflakes on the white paper, one at a time, in a pleasing arrangement. Overlap edges of the flakes. Cover each snowflake with a coat of starch before adding another.

4. Since some tissue paper colors bleed, fill the brush with starch and go over the entire surface of the collage, while wet, painting in only one direction to even out the colors and to make more attractive.

VARIATIONS: Try cutting other shapes and applying to different kinds of background papers such as wallpaper or newspaper for interesting effects.

layered snowflakes to hang

MATERIALS:

(3) 9" x 9" squares of tissue paper, all the same or different colors

piece of wax paper

liquid starch in a small container

scissors, paint brush

string or thread

DISCOVERY STEPS:

1. Fold each square of tissue paper in the following manner to prepare for cutting snowflakes:

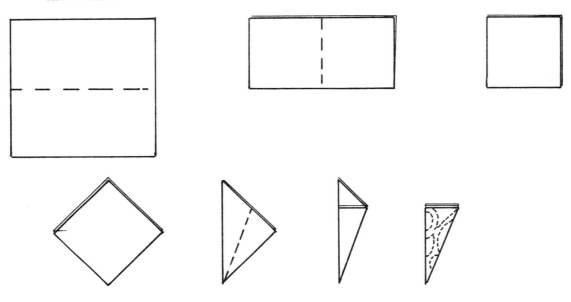

2. Place the piece of wax paper on top of a piece of newspaper.

3. Paint the wax paper with a coat of starch. Place one snowflake on this. Cover with starch. Place the second snowflake on top of the first and cover with starch. Place the third snowflake on top and cover it with starch. Paint carefully, gently as the snowflakes are fragile.

4. Let the tissue dry thoroughly, overnight if possible. When the tissue is dry the wax paper will peel away, leaving a stiff layered tissue snowflake. String with thread to hang.

MATERIALS:

scraps of tissue paper, all colors

liquid starch in a small container

scissors, paint brush

large piece of wax paper

string or thread, needle

lump of clay, coat hanger

newspaper

DISCOVERY STEPS:

1. Cover working surface with newspaper. Place the piece of wax paper on the center. Cut or tear the scraps of tissue into pieces of all sizes and shapes.

2. Using the paint brush, cover the wax paper with a coat of starch. It will not cover evenly but this will be remedied when the tissue is applied.

3. Place one piece of tissue paper at a time on the wax paper and cover with starch. The pieces can be picked up with the tip of the brush. *Overlap* the pieces of tissue paper, and continue until the entire piece of wax paper has two or three layers of tissue paper.

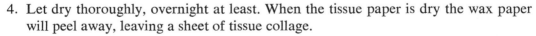

4. Let dry thoroughly, overnight at least. When the tissue paper is dry the wax paper will peel away, leaving a sheet of tissue collage.

5. Stretch the coat hanger and bend into a curved shape. Place one end in a lump of clay for a base.

6. Cut the tissue collage into shapes: butterflies, fish, flowers, etc. Using the needle and thread, add a string to each shape, making sure it is long enough to leave room to tie to the wire.

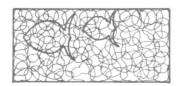

MATERIALS:

(1) piece of facial tissue, 2-ply

piece of wax paper, larger than facial tissue

colored tissue paper scraps

flat dried weeds (or flowers, ferns)

scissors and soft bristle paint brush

liquid starch in a small container

newspaper for working surface

DISCOVERY STEPS:

1. Spread newspaper on working surface. Place the piece of wax paper on the center of the newspaper.

2. Paint the surface of the wax paper with liquid starch. Arrange cut or torn pieces of colored tissue paper on the wax paper in any manner desired, covering each piece with liquid starch. Arrange the dried weeds on top of the tissue paper design. Cover the weeds with starch.

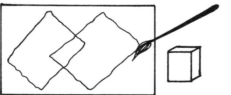

3. Separate the 2-ply tissue into two single pieces. Place one piece on the top of the design on wax paper, putting one edge of the facial tissue along the top of the wax paper, securing with starch. Pull the opposite edge until it is taut. Go over the design and press down. Use a brush or sponge to cover the surface of the facial tissue with starch.

4. If one piece of facial tissue is not big enough, add the second piece, overlapping ¼″ where they meet.

5. Let dry thoroughly. Coat front with protective covering, any desired.

parchment paper

MATERIALS:

(1) 2-ply facial tissue

piece of wax paper a little larger than facial tissue

colored tissue paper scraps

scissors and paint brush

small container of liquid starch

newspapers

DISCOVERY STEPS:

1. Spread newspaper on working surface. Place piece of wax paper on center of newspaper.

2. Paint the surface of the wax paper with liquid starch. Separate the 2-ply facial tissue into two pieces. Lay one piece on the starch-coated wax paper. Cover the piece of facial tissue with liquid starch, painting from the middle to the outside edges.

3. Place the torn tissue paper shapes on top of the starch-coated piece of facial tissue. Paint starch carefully on the tissue shapes.

4. Place the second piece of facial tissue on top of the tissue design and paint over with starch, again painting from the middle to the outside edges.

5. When the paper is dry, peel away the piece of wax paper. Mount on construction paper or simply trim edges and hang in window so the light will shine through.

MATERIALS:

tissue paper—variety of colors

(2) pieces of wax paper, same size

(2) 2″ x 12″ pieces of construction paper for trim

(1) piece of construction paper, same size as wax paper

warm iron, newspaper to iron on

(1) piece of yarn

DISCOVERY STEPS:

1. Place one piece of wax paper on top of the piece of construction paper. The construction paper will give support to the wax paper when moving it from the working surface to where it will be ironed.

2. Create a picture or design on the wax paper with torn pieces of tissue paper. Do not use scissors.

   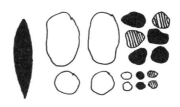

3. When the design or picture is completed, place the second piece of wax paper on top of the tissue paper. Place on a pad of newspapers and lay a single sheet of newspaper on top of the wax paper. Iron over the top, using a low or medium temperature. This will seal the tissue paper between the layers of wax paper.

4. Trim the top and bottom edges of the transparencies with 2″ wide strips of construction paper and hang with yarn if desired. They look great hung in the windows so that the light shines through.

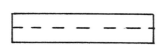 

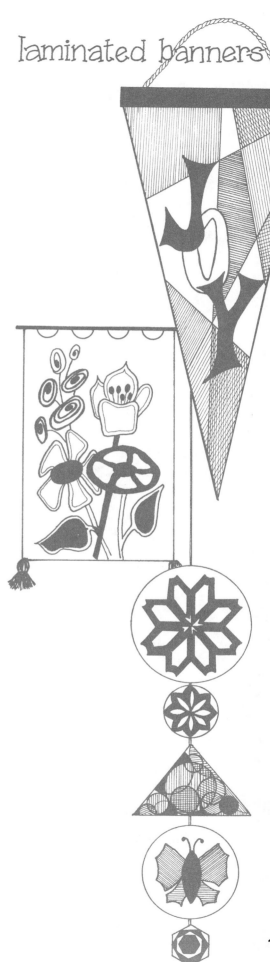

MATERIALS:

good quality wax paper

wax crayons

old iron

tissue paper, all colors

assorted string, sequins, glitter

scissors and white glue

construction paper

newspapers

DISCOVERY STEPS:

1. Place a sheet of wax paper the size desired on several thick layers of newspaper.

2. Cut out tissue shapes and lay on the wax paper.

3. Add other items such as sequins, glitter, pieces of scraped crayon, sprinkling over tissue.

4. Place a second sheet of wax paper on top of the arrangement.

5. Iron the entire design only once or twice with a medium-hot iron. Too much ironing can remove so much of the wax that there will not be enough left to seal the transparency.

6. Cools instantly. Add border at top and bottom using construction paper, yarn, braid, etc.

7. Display where the light will shine through.

HINTS:

· a pile of newspaper thick enough so the heat won't penetrate to the surface below makes a fine ironing surface;

· because of the size and length, make the banner where it can be ironed without moving.

MATERIALS:

(2) 20″ x 30″ tissue paper, white or light color

old crayons

vegetable grater

newspapers, cardboard

warm iron

DISCOVERY STEPS:

1. Using the vegetable grater, make shavings with the old crayons. Use only one or two colors.

2. Sprinkle the crayon shavings on one piece of tissue paper. These can be sprinkled in particular areas, patterns or designs if desired or scattered all over the paper.

3. Place the tissue on a thick pad of newspapers.

4. Place the second sheet of tissue paper on top of the crayon shavings. Put a single sheet of newspaper on top of the tissue paper. This will help the iron slide easily and hold the tissue paper still. Iron with a warm iron—just long enough to melt the wax without making the colors muddy.

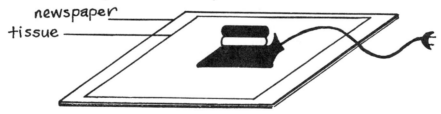

5. Remove the newspaper. Take the two pieces of tissue paper and quickly pull apart. If the melted crayon gets cold and hard it is possible that areas of melted crayon may pull apart entirely from one sheet or the other.

HINTS:

· use a piece of cardboard under the tissue paper when carrying it to the ironing area.

· both pieces of tissue paper may be the same color or each may be a different color.

· try using two colors of crayons that will produce a third color when they melt together: red and yellow, blue and yellow or red and blue.

MATERIALS:

black construction paper,
4½″ x 6″ (2 for each object)

colored tissue paper

needle and thread

paste or glue and scissors

reeds, straws or sticks on
which to suspend objects

DISCOVERY STEPS:

1. Fold two pieces of the black construction paper in half, lengthwise. Cut out half the shape of a butterfly. (You may wish to pencil the shape in before cutting.)

2. While the paper is still folded, cut into the wing shapes and cut out center sections. (See arrows.)

3. Unfold the shapes, paste or glue one side of one shape and lay it on the tissue paper. Put paste or glue on the other shape and attach to the other side of the tissue paper right behind the other shape so that they match exactly, back to back.

4. Trim the extra tissue paper away when the paste or glue is dry.

5. Using the needle and thread, attach the shapes to the sticks. You can use more than three shapes, making the mobile as simple or complex as desired.

6. It is possible to make many other mobile shapes with tissue paper in-between, following the same steps.

    a. Fold two pieces of construction paper the same size and cut out a shape.

    b. Cut into the shape and cut the center out while it is still folded.

    c. Open shapes, put on paste and place back to back, one on each side of the tissue paper.

    d. Trim away the excess tissue paper when the paste is dry.

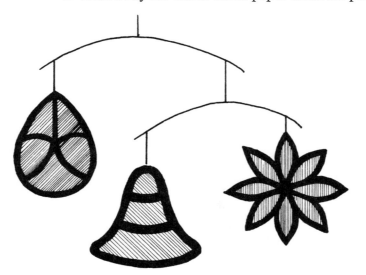 

window transparencies

MATERIALS:

(1) 9″ x 12″ black construction paper

pieces of colored construction paper

scissors

pencil

white glue or paste

DISCOVERY STEPS:

1. Fold the black construction paper in half, lengthwise. Draw a ½″ border around the open edges.

2. Draw a Christmas tree (or any shape) inside the border and a triangle inside each branch section. Join each branch section to the ½″ border with a double line.

3. Leaving the paper folded, cut out all the spaces around the double-lined design.

4. Open out the design and fill in the open spaces with colored tissue paper. Lay a piece of tissue paper on top of the hole to be covered and draw around the space, leaving a small border for gluing. Keep the design symmetrical by gluing the same color tissue in the matching spaces.

a bouquet

MATERIALS:

(9) 5″ x 5″ squares of tissue, 3 squares of 3 colors each

(3) pieces of string

scraps of green tissue for leaves

scissors and paste or glue

(1) 9″ paper doily, ribbon, or yarn

DISCOVERY STEPS:

1. Separate the tissue squares into three stacks containing three squares of tissue, three different colors.

2. Fold each stack of tissue together, accordian style, like a fan. Tie a piece of string around the middle of each fan. *Do not tie too tightly or gather the tissue.*

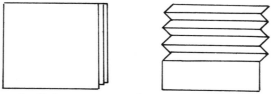

3. Round off the corners and spread out like a fan.

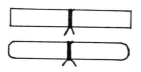 

4. Carefully separate each layer of tissue by pulling up gently to the string, fluff out.

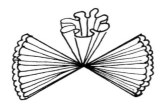 

5. Attach a pipe cleaner to the string holding the flower together. Cut leaves from the green tissue scraps and paste or glue to the stem near the flower.

6. Put a hole in the center of the paper doily. Put stems through holes. Secure doily to stems with tape. Add ribbon.

MATERIALS:

a bleached design

(1) 9" x 12" white construction paper

(1) 9" x 12" tissue paper, any color

small pieces of tissue paper, many colors

scissors, paint brush

liquid starch in a small container

Q-tips (sticks with cotton on end)

small amount of liquid bleach in
a sturdy container

DISCOVERY STEPS:

1. Place the 9" x 12" colored tissue paper on a layer of newspaper. Dip the end of the Q-tip in liquid bleach. Draw on the tissue paper with the Q-tip; dip in the bleach whenever necessary. Draw designs, patterns, shapes. The bleach will take the color out of the tissue paper.

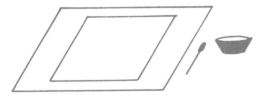  

2. While the tissue paper with the bleach is drying apply the small pieces of tissue paper to the 9" x 12" white construction paper. Paint the white paper with a layer of starch. Place the small pieces of tissue on the paper, leaving parts of the white paper showing. Cover each piece with starch.

3. Place the tissue paper with the bleached design on top of the white paper with the tissue pieces, carefully lowering into place, patting gently. Cover the entire design with a coat of starch. Let dry thoroughly.

tissue paper with
   bleach design

white paper with
   tissue design

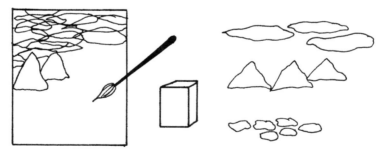

MATERIALS:

dried weeds—long, thin, feathery

4″ x 4″ squares of tissue paper:
light blue, shades of green, browns,
and yellows

white glue and water, ½ and ½

paint brush

9″ x 12″ heavy white paper

DISCOVERY STEPS:

1. Tear the squares of tisue paper into pieces of various sizes.

2. Paint the 9″ x 12″ heavy white paper with a coat of the glue mixture. Then put on some of the pieces of tissue paper, covering each piece with a coat of the glue mixture. (Keep in mind a landscape, putting the blue tissue at the top of the paper for sky and the other colors lower to give the impression of land, etc.

3. Make sure the entire paper has a good coat of the glue mixture and then arrange the dried weeds in a desired pattern over the tissue.

4. Cover each piece of tissue paper with the glue mixture and place over the dried weeds. Put on several layers of tissue.

MATERIALS:

(1) wire coat hanger

(2) 15″ squares of tissue paper, color of creature to be made

scraps of construction paper to decorate

scissors and paste or glue

DISCOVERY STEPS:

1. Holding the top of the hanger with one hand, pull the bottom of the hanger with the other hand to make a diamond shape. Pull around edges to shape the wire into a circular shape.

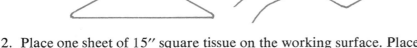

2. Place one sheet of 15″ square tissue on the working surface. Place the hanger shape on top. Trace around the outside of the wire with a pencil onto the tissue paper.

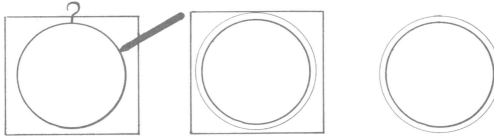

3. Place the second sheet underneath and cut out the shape, leaving a one-inch border.

4. Put paste or glue all around the edge of one piece of tissue paper. Then lay the hanger on top and put the second sheet of tissue on top. Press the edges gently, all the way around, sealing the hanger between the two pieces of tissue.

5. Using construction paper cut features, and so forth. The following illustrations will provide some ideas:

MATERIALS:

tissue paper, large sheets,
20″ x 30″

white glue, scissors

liquid starch, paint brush

string

thin strips of wood, reeds,
or the bamboo strips from an old
bamboo shade

scraps of cloth for tail

DISCOVERY STEPS:

1. Depending on the number of equal length sticks used, a great variety of shapes can
   be created for the framework of the kite. The following illustrations will provide
   ideas for two-stick, three-stick, and four-stick kites.

 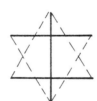  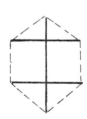

2. After deciding on the basic shape, glue and bind the sticks together. Notch (cut
   slits) the ends of the sticks and bind the ends with string for strength. Attach the
   string frame.

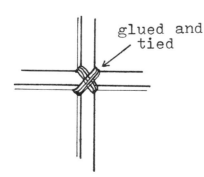

glued and
tied

notched

bind and tie
string around
each end below
notch.

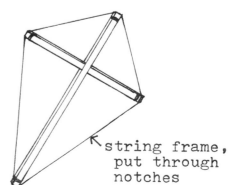

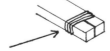

string frame,
put through
notches

58

3. Lay the kite frame on a piece of tissue paper and draw lightly around it with a pencil. Cut out, allowing a one-inch border all the way around. Cut out the corners as shown.

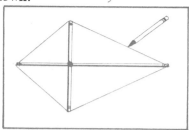

4. Decorate the tissue covering with other pieces of tissue using liquid starch and a paint brush. Add details with crayons or tempera paint.

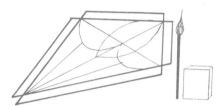
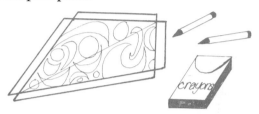

5. Place the kite frame on the dry tissue covering. Put glue or paste on the 1″ border and fold over the string frame. Make sure all edges are securely pasted down.

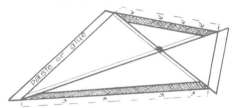

6. Attach the bow string across the width of the back of the kite as shown. Attach the string brindle across front of the kite as shown, as well as the flying string.

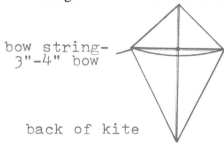
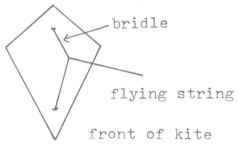

bow string—
3″-4″ bow

back of kite

bridle

flying string

front of kite

7. The tail for the kite can be made with scraps of cloth. The tail helps to keep the bottom of the kite at the bottom by acting as a balance. It is necessary to experiment with the length of the tail, so start with a long tail and cut to the length that gives the best results.

HINTS: Try using wrapping paper, large thin sheets of plastic, and other materials for the covering of the kite.

MATERIALS:

(1) piece of cardboard or chipboard of desired size

piece of foil, larger than cardboard

scraps of tissue paper

small container

scissors and white glue

masking tape

DISCOVERY STEPS:

1. Lay the foil on the table, shiny side down. Place the cardboard in the center. Fold the corners of the foil over and secure with tape. Then fold the side and end edges over and secure with tape. Turn over.

2. Make a mixture of glue and water in the small container, two parts glue to one part water. Paint the entire surface of the foil with the glue mixture. Add tissue shapes, designs or patterns, painting some of the glue mixture on top of each as it is put in place.

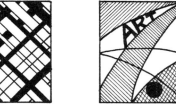

3. Finish by painting the entire surface of the decorated foil with a coat of the glue mixture. Let dry.

SUGGESTIONS:

—These make beautiful covers for notebooks.

—Try cutting Christmas ornament shapes from thin cardboard, covering with foil and decorating with tissue—absolutely beautiful.

MATERIALS:

a balloon, any size desired

tissue paper, all colors

liquid starch in a small container

small container to rest balloon
on while applying tissue

#12 watercolor paint brush

decorating materials for inside and
outside of egg: yarn, green grass, etc.

white glue to attach decorations

a tissue egg to hang

DISCOVERY STEPS:

1. Blow up balloon and *tie securely*.

2. Tear tissue into pieces that are medium in size. Pieces too large will wrinkle and be difficult to apply to balloon.

3. Using the paint brush, apply a coat of starch to an area of the balloon surface. Pick up pieces of tissue with the tip of the paint brush and put on the balloon. Cover each piece with liquid starch. Continue, covering the entire surface of the balloon several times, all pieces of tissue overlapping. Put many layers of tissue around the neck of the balloon as this will support the hanging egg. Let dry overnight or several days.

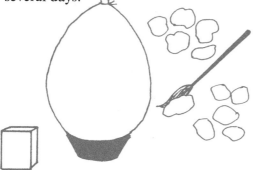

extra layers of tissue for strength.

4. Decide where the hole in the egg is to be. Make a cut with the scissors. Cut a circle. Take out the balloon.

5. Use a piece of roving or yarn to hang the egg. Put a large knot at one end and push the other end through the hole from the inside.

6. Decorate the outside of the egg; yarn, ribbon, rickrack, etc. can be glued around the hole in the egg and all over the surface. Sequins, felt flowers or anything else desired can be added.

tissue and wood plaques

MATERIALS:

    tissue paper, desired colors, various sizes (scraps too)

    white glue

    small container, scissors, paint brush

    piece of wood,* ¼″ to ⅝″ thick

    gro-grain ribbon, shellac, varnish or gloss medium, picture hook or ring

DISCOVERY STEPS:

1. Using the various pieces of tissue paper, cut out simple shapes. Experiment by arranging the shapes on a piece of paper the same size as the piece of wood. The background can be left plain or covered with pieces of tissue paper.

2. Make a mixture of 2 parts glue to 1 part of water in a small container.

3. Paint the surface of the wood with the glue mixture. Transfer the tissue pieces one at a time, from the paper to the wood, covering each piece with the glue mixture after it is placed on the wood. Let dry.

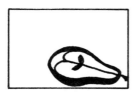 

4. When the picture is dry add details and accents with black marking pens or black paint.

5. To finish, paint the surface of the plaque with shellac, varnish or gloss medium. If black marking pens have been used to add details then *spray,* don't paint, so they won't smear.

6. Gro-grain ribbon can be glued to the outside edge of the wood and a picture hook or ring can be added for hanging.

* Before applying the tissue designs, the surface of the wood can be finished by using one of the following techniques:

1. Paint entire plaque with water or oil base paint, by hand or using spray paint.

2. Rub the surface of the wood with paste shoe polish to give an antique look.

3. Leave it the natural color, sanded very smoothly.

MATERIALS:

tissue paper, desired colors

white glue

small container, scissors, paint brush

piece of wood

dried seeds, beans, cereals

ribbon, shellac, varnish or gloss medium, picture hook or ring

seeds and bottles

DISCOVERY STEPS:

1. Cut bottle shapes from tissue paper. Each bottle can be a different shape or different size of the same shape. Arrange on a piece of newsprint to get an idea of placement, etc. More pieces of tissue can be added to create interest and to tie the composition together.

2. Make a mixture of 2 parts glue to 1 part water in the small container.

3. Paint the surface of the wood with the glue mixture. Transfer the tissue pieces, one at a time, from the newsprint to the wood, covering each piece with the glue mixture after it is placed on the wood. Let dry thoroughly.

 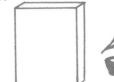

4. Using straight white glue, add dried beans, peas, seeds or cereals on the bottle shapes, giving the impression of partially filled bottles.

5. To finish, paint the surface of the plaque with shellac, varnish or gloss medium. Ribbon can be glued to the outside edge and a picture hook or ring can be added for hanging.

* Before applying the tissue bottles, the surface of the wood can be finished using one of several techniques:

1. Paint entire plaque with water or oil base paint, by brush or with spray paint.

2. Rub the surface of the wood with paste shoe polish to give an antique look.

3. Leave it the natural color (especially if using scrap paneling).

pretty and useful

MATERIALS:

scraps of tissue paper or pieces
cut into various shapes

liquid starch in a small container

bottle, box, tin can or jar

paint brush, scissors

gesso or latex paint *

shellac, varnish, gloss medium
or clear plastic spray

DISCOVERY STEPS:

* 1. Select a bottle, jar, box, or tin can. If the container has printing on it, first apply a
coat of gesso or latex paint and let dry. This will provide an opaque surface.

2. Tear or cut the tissue paper into small pieces.

3. Apply pieces of tissue paper to chosen container, using the liquid starch and paint
brush. Paint a small portion of the surface of the container with starch, put on
pieces of tissue and cover with starch. Cover the entire surface in this manner.

4. After the tissue and starch have dried, the container can be decorated with yarn
or string, secured with white glue.

5. To make durable and waterproof, cover the entire surface with shellac, varnish,
gloss medium, or clear plastic spray.

SUGGESTIONS: A marvelous quick fun way to make unsightly objects useful and
pretty. Boxes can be used for files, storage, personal objects. Flowers can be added
to the bottles. The tin cans can be used as pencil holders, for scissors, paint brushes,
or anything else you can think of.

6716